# The Project Sponsor Guide

# The Project Sponsor Guide

**Neil Love**
**Joan Brant-Love**

Project Management Institute

**Library of Congress Cataloging-in-Publication Data**

Love, Neil A., 1944–

    The project sponsor guide / Neil Love, Joan Brant-Love.

       p.     cm.

    ISBN: 1-880410-15-X (alk. paper)

    1. Group problem solving.   2. Group relations training.   3. Teams in the workplace.
4. Industrial project management.   I. Brant-Love, Joan, 1937–.  II. Title.


HD30.29 .L677 2000

658.4'036 – – dc21                              00–023371

                                               CIP


ISBN: 1-880410-15-X

Published by: Project Management Institute, Inc.
              Four Campus Boulevard
              Newtown Square, Pennsylvania 19073-3299 USA
              Phone: 610-356-4600 or Visit our website: www.pmi.org

10   9   8   7   6   5   4   3   2   1

# Contents

# Introduction

## Purpose

Project sponsors can have a tremendous impact on the success of key projects. However, in reality, they miss the mark and are often uninvolved or overinvolved and confused about their role.

The purpose of this guide is to help managers add value as sponsors of cross-functional projects including product development projects, information system projects, organizational change projects, and process improvement projects.

Section I explains the roles of the project sponsor as mentor, catalyst, motivator, barrier buster, boundary manager, and liaison to senior management. Key tasks of the project sponsor are explained, including how to effectively set up a project team and how to support the team throughout the project cycle.

Section II identifies over twenty common project team problems that arise, and provides alternate solutions for dealing with them.

The Appendix provides some helpful tools to increase team effectiveness and therefore project performance.

## Intended Audience

*The Project Sponsor Guide* is intended for executives and managers who will be, or are, sponsors of a project, particularly cross-functional projects. It is also helpful reading for facilitators and project leaders.

# Project Sponsor Roles and Activities

## Project Sponsor Roles

Project teams often fail because they do not have adequate management involvement, guidance, and support. A project sponsor can fill this void, especially on important cross-functional projects.

A project sponsor usually is of higher rank than team members. For strategically important efforts, the project sponsor should be a senior executive.

Following is a brief description of what the project sponsor does in each role.

### MENTOR

Increases the confidence of the project leader.
Helps the project leader understand the full
business context of project decisions. Improves the
project leader's leadership and problem-solving
skills.

### CATALYST

Stimulates the thinking and perspectives of the
project leader. Challenges assumptions. Plays
*devil's advocate* to help the project leader see more
options/reactions, and raises the level of thinking
of the project leader.

### CHEERLEADER

Helps the project leader stay motivated and deal
with team issues. Occasionally directly helps the
team members stay motivated through *pep talks*
and celebrations. Reminds the project leader and
the team of the importance of the mission.

### Barrier Buster

Knocks down barriers that are beyond the control of the project leader or project team. Barriers can include nonsupportive managers of team members, resource problems, team member availability problems, or lack of tools/equipment/facilities/software needed by the team.

### Boundary Manager

Keeps executives, managers, and professionals from meddling or interfering with the team's progress. Protects the team from unnecessary interactions with others or unnecessary reporting to others. Lets the team perform within the boundaries of the agreed-to team mission and contract.

### Senior Management Liaison

Before establishing a team, the project sponsor briefs the organization's senior leadership group on the planned team's mission, desired team members, and any constraints on the project. As the team moves through the project life cycle, the project sponsor periodically communicates to management the team's progress to date, and asks for help on issues beyond the control or influence of the project sponsor.

## Project Leader Role

A project leader can be selected by the team itself or by the project sponsor. It is generally most straightforward for the project sponsor to select the project leader. If there are politics involved, the project sponsor can always indicate that the project leader role will be rotated over time.

The project leader should be a respected, proven employee of the organization. This individual should have effective planning, communication, influence, problem-solving, and meeting-management skills.

Ideally, the project leader would have experience working with customers and would have worked in several functions in the organization, which would enable the project leader to facilitate *businesswide* thinking. In addition, the team will more quickly accept the project leader's guidance.

The project leader is charged with being the communication link between the team and the project sponsor. Of course, the project leader has many other responsibilities, including planning and coordinating the team's work and facilitating its progress.

## Initial Project Sponsor Activities

Following are some typical tasks that a project
sponsor performs when setting up a project team.

- ❑ Develops initial draft of team mission, goals,
  and constraints.
- ❑ Identifies appropriate team members.
- ❑ Gets buy-in from managers of team members.
- ❑ Gets buy-in from team members.
- ❑ Communicates importance of project mission.
- ❑ Helps refine team mission and goals.
- ❑ Identifies deficiencies in project plan.
- ❑ Gets senior management buy-in to team
  mission and goals.

## Ongoing Project Sponsor Activities

Working with the project leader, the project sponsor keeps abreast of team progress in the following ways.

### RESOURCES/SUPPORT

- ❑ Challenges thinking.
- ❑ Provides needed resources.

### PROGRESS REVIEWS

- ❑ Reviews progress of team with project leader.
- ❑ Occasionally attends the end of team meetings to hear progress.
- ❑ Examines the thoroughness and *reality* of the project plan.

### MOTIVATION

- ❑ Helps project leader and team members see what they have accomplished.
- ❑ Cheers the project leader and team when the going is tough.
- ❑ Ensures that the team celebrates progress milestones and successes.
- ❑ Encourages the team to celebrate improvements in how it operates.

## TEAM MEETING IMPROVEMENT

- ❑ Encourages/demands use of tools and methodologies.
- ❑ Inquires about the clarity of and consensus (see Appendix) agreement on the team mission.
- ❑ Asks if ground rules are being followed when problems arise.
- ❑ Encourages good meeting management practices (agenda, action items, ground rules, timekeeper and recorder assigned, and so on).
- ❑ Provides a skilled facilitator when the team is *over its head*.
- ❑ Tests to see if true consensus (see Appendix) has been reached on key decisions.
- ❑ Assesses if meetings are too short or too long.
- ❑ Asks what trends are emerging during the meetings.

## Issue Resolution

- ❑ Deals with *unavailable* team members.
- ❑ Breaks down functional barriers.
- ❑ Gets help from senior management.
- ❑ Ensures that appropriate project management tools are being used.

Projects sponsors can be helpful in two especially high-leverage ways.

*Ensuring team member attendance.* Ensure that managers allow their team members to get to meetings on time. This allows the meeting to begin on time and end on schedule.

One way to do this is to ask each manager to assign a person to take over when a team member leaves for a meeting. Without this in place, the team member will feel compelled to finish work before leaving, or be distracted during team meetings thinking about the work not getting done and about falling behind

*Preventing team meeting interruptions.* Tell managers and employees not to interrupt team meetings, even for "quick questions." Meeting interruptions are unsettling and disorienting to the team member called out of the meeting, as well as to the remaining team members.

When a team member leaves, the team stops and waits until the situation is settled. By their very nature, teams cannot effectively move ahead without everyone being present and involved.

## Other Project Team Support

The project sponsor ensures that the team is given adequate support to be successful. In addition to the support that the project sponsor directly provides, this also often includes support through the following roles.

### TRAINER

A trainer can help the team develop needed skills in teamwork and the use of appropriate processes and tools. This training would likely involve sixteen to twenty-four hours per team. It could be held as a two to three-day training event, or better yet be provided in *just-in-time* half-day sessions held every one or two weeks until completed.

### FACILITATOR

Once teams have been trained, a facilitator helps team members work together more effectively during meetings, and coaches with regard to the use of meeting and project management tools. After several meetings, the facilitator should be able to withdraw from attending meetings and then be on call as needed for special situations (e.g., high team conflict, advanced project management tools).

## MEETING ROOM

Teams need access to a meeting room that is convenient, quiet, and adequate in size. They should have priority over meeting space in most cases. Team meetings require flipcharts and overhead projectors. A laptop computer should be provided with word processing and spreadsheet capabilities, so that the team can type meeting notes and agendas and analyze some data without management information system (MIS) help.

## MATERIALS

Teams may need to purchase training materials, quick reference guides, analysis software, and office supplies. Management should provide a budget for these items.

## Management Information System/Desktop Publishing Support

Teams may need MIS support to gather, analyze, and report data. Desktop publishing support may also be needed for creating surveys, data collection forms, memos, and presentation materials. An internal group or external firm could provide this support.

## Consultant Support

A team may need analytical support from an expert in survey design or advanced analytical tools such as QFD, design of experiments, and so forth. This person could be an assigned staff person or an external consultant. A team could require sixteen to forty hours of consultant support.

## Selecting Project Team Members

One of the most important contributions of the project sponsor is to carefully select the project team members (sometimes in conjunction with the project leader). If this is done right, the odds of project success are greatly increased. To do this, the following success factors should be considered.

### TEAM SIZE

Try to keep the core team size to five to seven people. More than seven people creates challenging consensus (see Appendix) building and communication demands. Teams smaller than five people may result in inadequate perspective or limited innovation.

### PICKING THE RIGHT TEAM MEMBERS

Identify what groups should be represented on the team. Then identify individuals who have not only the functional/technical skills and knowledge, but also are effective in working with people and participating in meetings. Consider suppliers and customer representatives as team members when appropriate.

## FINAL SELECTION

Find out if the people you identified would be interested in working on the team and might be available or made available.

Although managers can be members of project teams, employees close to the detailed work often provide better insights into the true work. Also, having one or more managers on a team of employees can sometimes negatively impact group dynamics.

## BUY-IN

Visit the manager of each team member candidate to explain the process, and get permission to recruit the manager's employee as a team member. Decide jointly whether you—as project sponsor— or the prospective team member's manager will visit the team member candidate to assess the employee's interest.

Then tell the project team candidate why he was selected. Be sure to explain to both the potential team member and his manager what is likely to be required of a team member (see Selecting and Resourcing a Team Project in this guide).

## Team Mission Buy-in

To start the team with the least resistance and to ensure team support by members' managers, the following process should be followed.

1. Project sponsor develops draft of team mission.
2. Project sponsor identifies departments that should be involved and the best team member candidates.
3. Project sponsor and candidates' managers agree on slate of candidates (see Selecting Project Team Members in this guide).
4. Project sponsor forms team and holds kickoff meeting to explain team mission and importance of the team's efforts.
5. Team refines its mission and develops initial project plan.
6. Project sponsor and senior management approve project goals and plan.

*The team must own the team goals and project plan, or they will just be going through the motions.*

# Initial Project Team Communications

### TEAM MEMBER MEMO

At least two weeks before the first team meeting, the project sponsor sends a memo to the team members (copying their managers), covering the following:

- ❑ Mission on which the team will be working
- ❑ Importance of the mission to the organization
- ❑ Reason that members were chosen to be on the team
- ❑ Responsibilities as team members
- ❑ Roles of project sponsor (to provide focus and resources, and to secure the cooperation of other managers)
- ❑ Invitation to a thirty-minute *project briefing*.

## PROJECT BRIEFING

A week or so before the first team meeting, the project sponsor holds a thirty-minute kickoff session, including the following on the agenda:

- ❑ Upbeat welcome to team
- ❑ Importance of team mission and success
- ❑ "What's in it" for team members
- ❑ Question-and-answer session on team mission
- ❑ Concerns/schedule conflicts of team members
- ❑ Next steps.

## Project Sponsor/Project Leader Interactions

It is important that the project sponsor and project leader meet regularly and frequently (ideally after every team meeting) to review both teamwork and team task issues.

A regularly scheduled time should be set for the project sponsor and project leader to meet. The length of the meeting can be as short as fifteen minutes—especially if these meetings are held after every team meeting.

Avoid the use of E-mail as the only method for communicating team status to the project sponsor. Interacting in person (or at least on the phone) allows the project sponsor to judge what is going on, and sense issues to raise. In this way, the project sponsor facilitates problem solving more quickly, and emerging problems will be identified and addressed early.

The project leader's tone of voice and body language often provide clues of issues not being raised, so in-person meetings are best.

## Project Sponsor/Team Interactions

It is important to keep in mind that the team is responsible for achieving its mission. The project sponsor is a resource serving as coach, motivator, mentor, thought stimulator, and barrier buster—but is not typically an active member of the team.

Attendance of project sponsors (or other new people) at team meetings will usually affect the openness and functioning of the team. The team members have developed how they work together, including behavior norms. When new people attend a meeting, it may also slow the team (e.g., explaining history, why things are being done the way they are, and so on).

The team should generally be left to run its own meetings without having a project sponsor present. However, there are occasions when a project sponsor should attend a team meeting (or a portion of a meeting). For instance, the project sponsor might attend the first team meeting to help the team understand its mission and discuss any questions. Also, the project sponsor might occasionally attend the last ten to fifteen minutes of a team meeting to hear directly about team progress. In rare cases, the project sponsor might insist on attending a meeting to resolve a team crisis that has been festering.

Care must be taken to keep ownership of analysis and recommendations within each team. An enthusiastic project sponsor may start doing the team members' job, thus demotivating them or start taking over their tasks or the project leader's tasks.

In essence, a project sponsor's job is delegating. The trick is to be clear on the terms. The project sponsor and project leader should have a clear agreement on how to interact, communicate, and ensure progress.

## EXCEPTIONS

There are situations when the project sponsor should perhaps take a more hands-on role in working with the team, such as when:

❑ The project leader is inexperienced in project management
❑ The project leader is uncomfortable in the project leader role
❑ There is strong interdepartmental conflict.

In these cases, the project sponsor may provide additional help by:

- ❑ Attending the first two to three meetings to act as co-chair
- ❑ Helping the team develop its team mission and project plan
- ❑ Meeting often with the project leader to coach and help develop (outside of the meetings)
- ❑ Dealing with some team issues (e.g., nonparticipating or troublesome team member).

With time, the team members and the project leader will be able to work mostly by themselves, and a more typical *resource-on-call* role for the project sponsor can be resumed.

## Reviewing Team Progress

A project sponsor should stay close to the team yet not dominate, interfere, or manipulate it. Reviewing team progress and issues is an important coaching skill that must be utilized.

In the first month or two, the project sponsor and project leader should meet within a few days after each meeting for at least fifteen minutes to thoroughly discuss:

- ❑ Team progress against plan
- ❑ Team issues resolved
- ❑ Current team issues
- ❑ Potential team issues
- ❑ Help needed.

It is critical to discuss teamwork issues as well as team task/results issues. These should be separate meetings, not combined with other topics.

With time, the meetings may be scheduled every two or three weeks, unless a problem arises.

The project sponsor communicates the information listed earlier to senior management, and requests any needed help.

It is very important that the five points listed are thoroughly discussed and reported, rather than saying, "Here's kinda where we're at. ... " This formality ensures accountability, motivation, and needed support.

A checklist may prove helpful for the project sponsor/project leader meetings.

### CHECKLIST

- ❑ How is the team working together?
- ❑ Did all team members attend the last meeting? If not, why not?
- ❑ What progress has been made since the last meeting?
- ❑ Is the team on its planned schedule?
- ❑ Are there any team-interaction or meeting-management issues?
- ❑ Are there true consensus (see Appendix) and support for the team's recent decisions or recommendations?

If there are team progress or interaction problems, ask the project leader:

- ☐ Is everyone participating (e.g., giving ideas, taking team assignments)?
- ☐ Are meetings starting and stopping on time?
- ☐ What has been coming up in the last two or three meeting-effectiveness checks? (See Appendix.)
- ☐ What is the mood of the team? Has it changed? When? What caused the change?
- ☐ Is the team enforcing its ground rules?
- ☐ What can the project sponsor do to help?

## Expanding Project Teams

Sometimes, as a project team progresses, the team discovers a need for the help of someone who is not currently on the team. This person typically is needed because of important insights, knowledge or skills, or a better understanding of the transactions between the various groups involved in the project.

### ALTERNATIVE APPROACHES

Basically, the project team and project sponsor have a few choices for how to obtain the insights and necessary input from the new person.

| Options | New Person's Role |
|---------|-------------------|
| Option 1 | Consultant to project team |
| Option 2 | Subteam member |
| Option 3 | Project team member |

*Option 1—Consultant to project team.* Have the project leader meet with the new person between team sessions to get the person's input, insights, and suggestions. The project leader then discusses these comments with the team, and the team decides what changes to make in the project plan.

**Pros**

Doesn't change team dynamics.

Team doesn't have to repeat discussions from prior meetings.

**Cons**

Takes additional time of the project leader.

*Option 2—Subteam member.* Create a subteam that includes one or more of the original team members, plus new people needed to fill missing knowledge or experience areas. Of course, the new people on the subteam may need to receive the same training that was provided to the team.

**Pros**

Doesn't change team dynamics.

Team doesn't have to repeat prior discussions.

**Cons**

Subteam's work may affect schedule.

*Option 3—Project team member.* If the earlier-mentioned approaches are inadequate or inappropriate, a new person may have to be added to the team. This is an important decision, and the team and project sponsor should carefully consider it. Have the team perform a pros-and-cons analysis and decide through consensus (see Appendix) if adding a new member is worth the price to be paid.

If the decision is made to add a new team member, carefully assimilate the person into the team. This includes educating the person on the team mission, the work done to date, the decisions made to date, and the reasons why. Any training that the team has had in project management or other areas must be provided to the new team member. Some team building must also be done, with the new member present.

### Pros

Get full insights/inputs needed real time.

### Cons

Team will have to repeat team building.
Team dynamics may be affected some to a lot.
Team will revisit decisions and work done to date.
May require facilitator to come to team meetings.

# Common Problems and What to Do About Them

The project sponsor role is a challenging and sometimes awkward job. As the team moves along, many issues come up with the team, the project leader, other managers, or even with you as project sponsor.

The following sections identify common problems that tend to come up, suggest possible causes, and provide some notions on what the project sponsor might do to help resolve issues.

When some of these issues arise, you may want to consider enlisting the aid of a consultant, facilitator, or a trainer, when appropriate.

## Impact of Environment

When a team is having trouble, it is always helpful to first consider if organizational crises or new projects are diverting time and attention and lowering the apparent priority and importance of the team project. For example, sudden negative profitability may result in layoffs, employees putting in much overtime, and so on.

You can also ask the team members what has changed, and then ask them to discuss how they can best move ahead.

## Team Problems

### TEAM MEMBER MISSING MEETINGS

*Situation.* Within a few weeks after a team starts, one member (or more) stops attending team meetings, or attends sporadically. This causes significant team productivity problems, and decisions are made without the valuable perspectives of the missing team member(s). Team energy and commitment also suffer, because loyal team members wonder about the importance of the project and why they should come if others aren't.

A project sponsor should quickly jump on this problem when it first occurs, not simply hope that it will work itself out.

#### Possible Causes

❑ Agreement from team member's manager was not solicited or gained before she was assigned to the team.

❑ Lack of true buy-in by the manager of the missing team member.

❑ Suppressed conflict between the missing team member and the team.

- Overworked team member.
- Missing team member does not believe that the team mission is important to him or to the company.
- No ground rule regarding accountability of team members to attend meetings or to reschedule if unavoidable conflicts arise.
- Team member or manager of team member does not realize the impact on the team when a member misses a team meeting.
- Manager of missing team member sends subtle signals that the team member should stay on the job.
- Guilt caused by team member's peers back on the job, as they feel that work is being dumped on them while the team member is gone.

**Things to Try**
- Add a ground rule on team attendance that requires advance notification if a member can't attend, so that rescheduling the meeting can be considered.
- Ask the project leader to contact the missing team member to find out why the team member is not coming to meetings.

- ❑ Talk to the project leader and facilitator to get their views on what should be done to get the missing team member to attend.
- ❑ Talk (gently) to the missing team member to see why she is not coming.
- ❑ Meet with the missing team member's manager to ask why he thinks the employee is not coming to team meetings.
- ❑ Ask for the manager's commitment to ensure that the team member will be encouraged to attend the team meetings.
- ❑ Problem solve with the manager if there are valid reasons why the team member can't attend (e.g., change priorities of projects, change day or time of team meetings, get additional resources or back-up personnel, and so forth).
- ❑ If the manager remains uncooperative, tell her that you will have to bring up the matter with her boss or with senior management to resolve the problem.
- ❑ Change the performance-appraisal system to include recognition for contributions to departmental and interdepartmental teams.

## SERIOUS TEAM MEMBER CONFLICT

*Situation.* Too much tension has developed between two or more team members, or the team has split into two camps.

### Possible Causes

❑ Not all team members were being heard in meetings.

❑ Team has not been reaching true consensus (see Appendix) when making decisions.

❑ Team members have been talking over the top of each other.

❑ Meeting-effectiveness checks (see Appendix) haven't been used at team meetings.

❑ In early stages, team members had not discussed how they would deal with conflict.

❑ Team members were not brainstorming ideas and then evaluating them. Instead, they were selling or presenting ideas as *the* idea. Or ideas were immediately agreed to or challenged before all ideas were heard.

❑ Team has not thoroughly discussed pros and cons of alternative ideas.

❑ Team member is being pressured by boss to sabotage/resist the team's progress or plans.

❑ Dominating or abrasive team member is setting off the bells of another team member.

### Things to Try

❑ Ask the project leader what has been hindering progress, or what the meeting-effectiveness checks (see Appendix) have been showing.

❑ Ask the project leader about both task and group dynamics behavior patterns of the team and individual members.

❑ Ask the project leader to put conflict management resolution on the next team meeting agenda.

❑ Ask the project leader to work with a facilitator to decide how to deal with and resolve the conflict.

❑ Assign a facilitator to the team to deal with the conflict.

❑ Temporarily assign an experienced conflict-management specialist to the team (while the regular facilitator observes).

- ❑ If the previous suggestions don't work, meet with the team to decide what has to be done to get the team moving again and stop the conflict.
- ❑ As a last resort, gracefully replace the troublesome team member(s) with perhaps new members from the same functional areas. (New-member orientation and team building will be needed to minimize the slowdown caused by assimilating new members.)

## OVERLY DEPENDENT TEAM

*Situation.* The team looks for too much direction from the project sponsor, especially when the sponsor attends team meetings.

### Possible Causes
- ❑ "Tell-me-what-to-do" organizational culture.
- ❑ Project sponsor is not utilizing participative management skills.
- ❑ High-level project sponsor in a hierarchically oriented culture.
- ❑ Team members are uncomfortable acting as an empowered or self-directed team.

- Project sponsor has a directing management style.

### Things to Try

- Ensure that the project leader knows that he is accountable for team direction.
- When team members ask for direction, the project sponsor should ask the team to discuss alternatives, pros and cons of each, and then decide what to do without the project sponsor.
- Assign a facilitator to work with the group to increase members' confidence and initiative.
- Attend only the first or last ten minutes of team meetings to see how the team is doing, where it is, and what issues have come up.
- Do not attend team meetings for a while.

## TEAM SKIPPING STEPS

*Situation.* Teams, in their rush to make progress, often skip over project planning or execution steps, or do an inadequate job on a given step.

**Possible Causes**

❑ Pressure for progress from the project sponsor or a team member.

❑ Team members are pressured by their managers to spend minimal time in team meetings.

❑ Not enough time is set aside for team meetings, or an insufficient number of team meetings are held.

❑ How to complete the step was forgotten after training was done.

❑ Training did not provide enough practice to develop skill and confidence.

❑ Team is not truly committed to the importance or benefit of the team mission.

❑ Team members don't believe that the tool or procedure used in the step is really helpful or practical.

**Things to Try**

❑ Ask the project leader what she thinks is causing the team to not fully use tools or procedures (e.g., too rushed, don't know the tool/step, low team commitment, and so on).

- Check how long team meetings are and how often they are held. If meetings are less than two hours, ask the team members (via the team leader) if they could hold longer or perhaps more frequent meetings.
- Provide a facilitator or trainer to refresh the team's memory about the tools or steps, and facilitate their use for a few meetings.
- Revisit the team's mission with members and check for buy-in. Adjust the mission or provide solutions to team member issues (i.e., boss/peers don't like me coming to these meetings).

## TEAM CONFLICT DURING PRESENTATIONS

*Situation.* In presenting their recommendations to the project sponsor, he senses that some members of the team are not fully behind the recommendations. Or, worse yet, when the team is presenting to the management team, members fall apart or argue during the meeting about their differences.

## Possible Causes

❑ Some team member(s) did not voice their concerns about an approach.

❑ Some team member(s) did not offer recommendations.

❑ All recommendations were not fully acknowledged by the team.

❑ Team did not fully discuss pros and cons of each approach.

❑ Hidden or open conflict in the team prevents the team from considering all ideas.

❑ True consensus (see Appendix) on recommendations was not reached.

## Things to Try

❑ Ensure that team members really understand what consensus (see Appendix) is and that they know how to be sure that they have it.

❑ Remind the team that it must reach consensus (see Appendix) on any recommendation that will be presented to management.

❑ Ask the team to list all ideas originally
considered (perhaps adding some new ones),
do a pros and cons analysis on all the ideas,
and have the team present its idea list and
pros/cons to the project sponsor.

## DYSFUNCTIONAL TEAM MEMBER

*Situation.* A team member is seriously disrupting
teamwork and team progress.

### Possible Causes
❑ Team member has a dominating or abrasive
style.
❑ "Angry-to-be-here" team member.
❑ Old wounds are surfacing between team
members.
❑ Disruptive team member is really reflecting
where the team as a group is.

### Things to Try
❑ Have the project leader or a facilitator work
with the team to surface and discuss issues that
have been unresolved (see Surfacing Issues
Technique in Appendix).

- ❑ Have the dysfunctional team member meet with the project sponsor, the team leader, or a facilitator. Ask the team member what she can do to help the team move along and work better. Members agree together on what will be done.
- ❑ As a last resort, if the team member is unwilling to try something new or does not do what she committed to try, it may be one of those rare cases when the member may have to leave the team.

## NEW TEAM MOVING ALONG TOO SLOWLY

*Situation.* A newly established team has had several meetings with good attendance and doesn't seem to have any conflicts, but is progressing much more slowly than other teams.

### Possible Causes
- ❑ "World hunger"-type team mission.
- ❑ Ambiguous mission statement.
- ❑ Team was not provided with a buy-in process for its mission.

- [ ] Team does not have consensus (see Appendix) on how it is going to move forward.
- [ ] Team does not have a near-term action plan for the next thirty to sixty days.
- [ ] Prevailing organizational culture is directive, and the team feels very uncomfortable acting in a more self-directed mode.
- [ ] Team does not sense any urgency for its project.
- [ ] Team members do not see what they will be getting out of the project. ("What's in it for me?")
- [ ] Team is not managing its meetings well (e.g., no agendas, ground rules not followed, points are made at great length).
- [ ] Most of the team members are more socially oriented, rather than task oriented.
- [ ] Overly polite team whose members feel uncomfortable offering or challenging ideas. (No conflict or low conflict is the norm.)

### Things to Try
- [ ] Discuss concerns with team members, and ask what they think is causing them to move at the current pace.

- ❑ Phase the project, starting with something doable and fairly quick (e.g., gather customer concerns and prioritize them in thirty days).
- ❑ Split the mission into two or more parts on which different teams or subteams will work. (Be on the lookout for redundant work and lack of a total systems view.)
- ❑ Communicate a sense of urgency to the project leader and the team.
- ❑ Establish a reasonable deliverable that the team must achieve in two weeks.
- ❑ Sequester team with a facilitator for three to five days, to accelerate progress and help the team become more task oriented, self-directed, and accepting of conflict.
- ❑ Have team members identify what they would like to get out of the project and what they think they will get out of it. Try to shape project work so that everyone gets something that they want.
- ❑ Explain to the team that polite people are good people, but to perform well, teams must hear all views clearly, discuss them candidly, and reach consensus.

❑ Have the project leader or a facilitator work with the team to surface and discuss issues that have been unresolved. (See Surfacing Issues Technique in Appendix.)

❑ As a last resort, add a project leader and/or one or two new team members with strong task orientation.

## PREVIOUSLY SUCCESSFUL TEAM BOGGING DOWN

*Situation.* A team has been moving along fairly well for quite a while, with only a few setbacks from which members recovered nicely. But this time, the team is just not going anywhere. After several meetings, no further progress has been made (e.g., no new decisions, analysis, or recommendations).

### Possible Causes

❑ Team is getting down on itself and not even celebrating small achievements, (e.g., teamwork improvements, quick actions taken, and accomplishment of project plan milestones).

- A power struggle has developed within the team.
- Team has lost sense of direction.
- Team members are realizing that the project is big and intimidating.
- The team now feels that the project is really not that important.
- Some significant organizational change or issue has come up that is diverting attention and/or time.
- Team members can no longer *live with* certain team behaviors, but don't confront the issues head on.
- The team may be nearing a recommendations deadline or a key implementation milestone and is fearful that management will disapprove.
- A manager has raised doubts about the project or its direction with a team member, and the doubt has now spread throughout the team.
- Team had felt empowered and supported, but management has let members down somehow.
- On high-stress, very challenging, or ambiguous projects, team burnout may be setting in.
- The team thinks that it is basically done.

### Things to Try

☐ Hold a celebration party for what the team has achieved, and give members a pep talk.

☐ Help the team create specific goals and milestones (which create urgency).

☐ Add a customer to the team.

☐ Have the project leader or a facilitator work with the team to surface and discuss unresolved issues. (See Surfacing Issues Technique in Appendix.)

☐ Ask the project leader what has changed in the last several weeks that may be affecting the team, or meet with the team as a whole to get its response to the same question.

☐ Ask the team what can be done to continue team progress.

☐ If the project is vital to the organization, consider sequestering the team members for several days with an excellent facilitator.

## Project Leader Problems

### PROJECT LEADER AVOIDS PROJECT SPONSOR

*Situation.* Meetings between the project leader and project sponsor have not been occurring regularly. The project leader seems unavailable or uninterested in having meetings.

#### Possible Causes

❑ Project leader is uncomfortable in the role.

❑ Project leader feels intimidated by the project sponsor.

❑ Project leader is very busy and feels that he can't take the time.

❑ Project leader's boss feels discomfort about her employee *reporting* to another manager.

❑ Project leader does not know how or when to initiate contact with project sponsor.

❑ Project leader is hesitant to report on negative behaviors of a team member.

❑ Project leader is afraid that project sponsor will be upset with team progress or direction.

- ❑ Project leader feels caught between the team's desires and the project sponsor (see next problem).
- ❑ Project sponsor and project leader have not reached true consensus (see Appendix) on a regular meeting schedule and agenda.
- ❑ Meetings with project sponsor are too lengthy or are confusing.
- ❑ Project sponsor is acting more like a boss than like a coach.
- ❑ Project sponsor has a hidden agenda, on which he wants the team to act, rather than helping the team objectively accomplish its goal.

**Things to Try**
- ❑ Project sponsor and project leader establish a schedule to meet regularly for a set length of time.
- ❑ Project sponsor mentors the project leader through new skill areas or through trying times.
- ❑ Project sponsor reminds the project leader that timely good and bad news is needed for two reasons. One, the project sponsor needs to know about issues, challenges, and setbacks, so that she knows when to provide help. (The

longer the delay, the harder it is to help.) Secondly, the organization is in a learning mode, and project leader input to the project sponsor will help future teams, project leaders, project sponsors, and managers of team members.

❑ Project sponsor objectively examines her agenda (e.g., "Implement my plan, not yours,") and recognizes the stress that it causes. She opens up to other suggestions and approaches suggested by the team and asks the team to conduct an objective pros-and-cons analysis on all ideas, solutions, and so forth.

❑ Project sponsor and project leader conduct meeting effectiveness checks at each of their meetings, and adjust next meeting as necessary (see Appendix).

❑ As a last resort, project leader role is graciously rotated to another team member, who may be more comfortable and capable in this capacity.

## PROJECT LEADER IN THE MIDDLE

*Situation.* A project leader feels squeezed between the team and project sponsor, because the team is heading one way and the project sponsor wants something else to happen. The team *beats up* on the project leader when he reports the project sponsor's viewpoints, and the project sponsor *beats up* on the project leader when reporting the team's viewpoints.

### Possible Causes

❑ Team's mission is not agreed to or clearly understood by the team or the project sponsor.

❑ Project sponsor does not acknowledge and express respect for the team's ideas reported by the project leader.

❑ Team does not know or appreciate the project leader's dilemma.

❑ Project leader presents project sponsor viewpoint in a way that troubles the team.

❑ Project sponsor has not been close enough to the team.

❑ Project sponsor or project leader training was not done, or was done insufficiently.

### Things to Try

☐ Invite a facilitator to meet with the team and the sponsoring manager to clarify roles of the team members, team leader, and project sponsor.

☐ Have a facilitator attend project leader/project sponsor meetings.

☐ Have a facilitator attend team meetings when the project leader is reporting the project sponsor's reactions to the team's activities.

☐ The project sponsor or a facilitator meets with the team to build agreement and commitment for the team mission and direction.

## PROJECT LEADER NOT WORKING OUT

*Situation.* A project leader has not been functioning well (e.g., inadequate project plan, no use of action items, unable to influence team direction or lead the team, not responsive to project sponsor requests).

### Possible Causes

☐ Project leader selection process didn't exist, or wasn't carefully thought out.

- Project leader was chosen on the basis of technical knowledge or functional experience, not project leader skills (e.g., project management, meeting management, interpersonal communication, and so on).
- Project sponsor preferred (most likely for control reasons) a person from her function over better project leader candidates.
- None of the team members were good project leader candidates.

### Things to Try

- Assign a facilitator to work with the team and one-on-one with the project leader.
- Place the project leader in an intensive two to three day project leader-training program.
- Project sponsor spends extra time coaching and developing the project leader.
- Split the project leader duties between the current project leader and other team member(s).
- Shift the project leader into a communications liaison role, and assign a facilitator to run a few meetings.

❑ Establish a policy of project leader rotation after one to three months of service.

## PROJECT LEADER BURNOUT

*Situation.* The project leader's spirit seems to have been dampening for some time now. The project leader doesn't exhibit the energy, creativeness, or resourcefulness that he once did in meetings with the project sponsor and the team. The project leader doesn't volunteer for team assignments and may even reject accepting them, or doesn't do them in as timely or thorough a manner as he once did.

### Possible Causes
❑ Work overload (own job, plus project leader role).
❑ Poor working relationship with project sponsor.
❑ Manager of project leader resents time spent by project leader on team activities.

### Things to Try
❑ Recognize project leader for work done.

- ❑ Have project leader pass some responsibilities to other team members.
- ❑ Give project leader some time off with pay.
- ❑ Rotate project leader position to another team member.
- ❑ Project sponsor meets with project leader's manager to discuss the problem, explore options, and solve problems.

***Note***: Beyond their regular jobs, project leaders carry an extended workload, which includes team meetings, planning and communicating about team meetings, and one-on-one meetings with the project sponsor and other managers or team members.

Extra work—compounded by the stress of trying to maintain good teamwork and relations with his own boss and the project sponsor (and sometimes even with family)—can result in the project leader resenting his predicament.

## Problems with Other Managers

### Unsupportive Manager

*Situation.* A manager of a team member is not allowing her employee to go to meetings or is indirectly punitive.

### Possible Causes

❑ When the team was set, the manager was not approached to explain the purpose and importance of the team and get her buy-in, allowing her employee to attend meetings.

❑ The team meetings have become longer or more frequent than was first explained.

❑ The team has been in operation longer than expected.

❑ Something has changed so that the manager can no longer afford the team member being away for some or all of the meetings.

❑ The manager does not believe in the team's mission or a team approach.

### Things to Try

❑ Meet with the manager to review the importance of the team and its mission to the organization.

❑ Try to understand her concerns. Solve problems and negotiate a win-win solution (e.g., set different meeting time, length, or frequency; help secure a backup person; and so forth).

❑ If that is not productive, tell the manager that you will have to speak to her boss or senior management to resolve the issue.

## MEDDLING MANAGER

*Situation.* A manager is frequently interacting with the project leader or a team member offering unsolicited or even unwanted suggestions on what the team should do or where it should be going.

### Possible Causes

❑ Manager doesn't realize the impact this has on the team.

❑ Manager is nervous that the team may uncover things that he doesn't want uncovered.

❑ Manager is very interested in the success of the team and perhaps may have wanted to be the project sponsor.

### Things to Try

❑ Meet with the manager to explain the mission of the team. Ask what questions he has about the team.
❑ Explain that the team should be shielded from too much external influence.
❑ Request that in the future the manager contact the project sponsor, rather than the project leader or team members, with questions or suggestions.
❑ If the manager continues to meddle, tell him that you will have to speak to his manager or to senior management about the situation.

### SABOTAGING MANAGER

*Situation.* A manager is undermining the team's mission, its performance, or its recommendations.

## Possible Causes

☐ Manager is operating with inaccurate or old data on the team.

☐ Manager doesn't want her employee taking time to be on the team.

☐ Manager sees the project as critical and has no faith in the project sponsor.

☐ Manager is in competition with the project sponsor for career gains.

☐ Manager is throwing acid on the whole project team concept.

☐ Manager has a history of working through others, rather than being direct.

## Things to Try

☐ Meet with the manager to ask what concerns he has about the team. Ask the manager to tell you directly about any of his concerns in the future.

☐ If the manager continues to sabotage, tell him that you will have to speak to his manager or to senior management about the situation.

## Threatened Manager

*Situation.* The manager of a project leader or team member is upset that her employee is *going around* her and meeting with a more senior-level manager, the project sponsor. The manager has insisted that the employee not do this again.

### Possible Causes
❑ The manager was not approached when the team was set, and doesn't understand that it is routine and expected that the team leader— and sometimes a team member or the entire team—will meet with the project sponsor.
❑ The manager feels threatened that her employee will say something that will get her into trouble.

### Things to Try
❑ Meet with the manager and explain how the team and sponsoring manager interactions work, and that the focus is on cross-functional issues, not issues in her department.
❑ Ask what concerns the manager has, and then deal with those concerns.

## Project Sponsor Problems

### TENDENCY TO OVERCONTROL

*Situation.* Project sponsor is overly directing the project team or project leader.

#### Possible Causes
- ❑ Project sponsor has an overcontrolling management style.
- ❑ The project is critical, and the project sponsor is nervous that this team may not be strong enough to be successful.
- ❑ Project sponsor wants to get the project rolling fast.
- ❑ Project sponsor is not comfortable with or committed to a team approach.

#### Things to Try
- ❑ Project sponsor asks for guidance from a facilitator.

- ❑ Sequester the team members with an outstanding facilitator for three to five days to build the necessary teamwork skills, quickly get team buy-in and clarity on its mission, and get the project going.
- ❑ Present your ideas to the project leader in more of a question format than a statement format. For example: "What are the pros and cons of this decision?" "In what ways could the team benefit by an outsider's opinion?"
- ❑ Project sponsor cools his jets for at least three to four meetings, then judges if any adjustments are needed.
- ❑ Talk to seasoned project sponsors, and ask what they did to deal with this situation.

## TOO CLOSE OR TOO FAR FROM TEAM

*Situation.* The project sponsor is struggling with the project sponsor role and is staying distant from the team, or is fluctuating back and forth, between being too close and too far away.

## Possible Causes

- ❑ Project sponsor not clear on the role.
- ❑ Project sponsor is reacting too quickly to setbacks or assuming that current success means that no trouble is brewing.
- ❑ Project sponsor's natural style is highly directive and she is overcompensating by staying distant from the team, but sometimes succumbs to her controlling style and overdirects.

## Things to Try

- ❑ Ask the project leader if the project sponsor has been too close or too distant from the team, and ask for suggestions.
- ❑ Meet with a facilitator to discuss ways to consistently be close enough, but not too close, to the team.
- ❑ Talk to seasoned project sponsors and ask what they did to deal with this situation.

## NOT ENOUGH TIME

*Situation.* Project sponsor is not able to spend time supporting the team by meeting with the project leader, attending team meetings, and so forth.

### Possible Causes
- [ ] Organizational crisis.
- [ ] Increased workload or duties.
- [ ] Project sponsor does not delegate effectively.
- [ ] Travel requirements of job.
- [ ] Project sponsor really prefers firefighting on other things that come up.
- [ ] Project sponsor's boss sees the team project as having a lower priority than other projects.

### Things to Try
- [ ] Delegate some managerial duties to subordinates.
- [ ] Empower the project leader to take on more responsibility for directing the team and team success.
- [ ] Assign a facilitator to the team, who contacts the project sponsor only when his input is needed.

- ❑ Ask another experienced project sponsor to take over for a while.
- ❑ Slow down the team meeting frequency.

## OVERBURDENED

*Situation.* The project sponsor is spending much more time than originally expected in supporting the team and the project leader.

### Possible Causes
- ❑ Project scope expanded.
- ❑ Data gathering has surfaced unexpected risk/complexity of the project.
- ❑ The project leader is not working out.
- ❑ Unexpected resistance from team members, their managers, or key stakeholders has surfaced.
- ❑ The urgency of the team's project has increased, and completion is needed sooner than expected.

### Things to Try

☐ Empower the project leader to take on more responsibility.

☐ Assign a facilitator to the team, who contacts the project sponsor only when her input is needed.

☐ Delegate regular management tasks to subordinates.

☐ Sequester the team with an outstanding facilitator for three to five days, to get the project going.

☐ Rotate the project leader.

### MANIPULATING THE TEAM

*Situation.* The project sponsor believes that he knows the right team approach or plan, and knowingly or unknowingly influences the team to do only what he wants.

## Possible Causes

☐ Project sponsor does not trust or see value in the team concept.

☐ To avoid the appearance of being self-serving, the project sponsor wants the team to present his idea.

## Things to Try

☐ Decide if project sponsor can function as one who will truly consider other recommendations made by the team.

☐ Examine the project sponsor's agenda (e.g., "Implement my plan, not yours."), and recognize the stress that it places on the team.

☐ Open up to other suggestions and approaches that the team may have, and ask the team to do an objective pros and cons analysis on all ideas, plans, and so on.

☐ Ask the team members if they will evaluate the project sponsor's suggestions and decide if they are acceptable. If the members buy in to the suggestions, ask them to help create an effective plan.

## Not Sharing Insights/Ideas

*Situation.* For fear of crowding the team, a project sponsor assumes that the team must explore everything from scratch. As a result, she holds back on insights (e.g., "What I see happening is. ... "), suggestions (e.g., "Do you think our suppliers could help?"), or resources (e.g., "What if I provided a known expert to speak to the team?").

### Possible Causes
- ❑ Project sponsor does not realize that she should occasionally provide a broad framework or perspective that will generate insights.
- ❑ Project sponsor does not understand that anything that saves time for the team can be helpful.

### Things to Try
- ❑ Ask the project leader if project sponsor has been too close or too distant from the team.
- ❑ Ask the project leader if he feels that the project sponsor's suggestions would help the team or derail it.

# Appendix

## Team Ground Rules

The way teams work in meetings can be productive or counterproductive. Team ground rules should be agreed to early by the team members. They represent the code of conduct for how team members will behave. Once adopted, all members should take responsibility for ensuring that team members follow all ground rules. Otherwise, the ground rules are quickly forgotten, and poor meeting behavior triumphs.

Listed below are some ground rules that a team could consider adopting. Given their own particular culture, most teams will want to pick or develop five or eight ground rules to use for their meetings.

- ❑ All team members are equal.
  - — Job titles and hierarchies are not relevant. In team meetings, all team members are treated as equals.
- ❑ All views are important.
  - — All team members contribute fully to the team in order to realize synergy and achieve thorough review of alternatives and lasting consensus decisions.
  - — Team members invite nonparticipating team members to give their opinions.
  - — If a team member is tending to dominate, remind him that other team members also need to be heard.
- ❑ Meetings start and stop on time.
  - — Meetings start and end at the scheduled times to eliminate negative impact on those members who are prompt.
  - — As a courtesy, anyone arriving late explains to the team the reason for the delay.
- ❑ Members commit to meetings.
  - — Team members attend all regularly scheduled meetings.

- Team members make their own managers aware of scheduled meetings so that arrangements for backup can be made.
- In the event of an unavoidable conflict, the affected member contacts the project leader ahead of the scheduled meeting, or leaves a message at the team meeting location.
- As a courtesy, any no-show explains the reason for nonattendance to the project leader promptly and to the whole team at the beginning of the next meeting.

❑ No side conversations.
- There are no side conversations while meetings are in session.
  Side conversations are distracting, add confusion, and send negative messages to other team members.

❑ Meeting interruptions for emergencies only.
- Every effort is made to ensure that team members are not interrupted by anyone from outside of meetings.
- A person called away informs the caller that he is in a meeting and asks if it would be possible to get back to the caller after the meeting.

— In the event of an emergency, a person called out of the meeting reports back to the team to inform the other members if, or for how long, he will be absent from the meeting. The team will then decide whether to take a break until the person returns, continue the meeting, or discontinue the meeting.

❑ All *electronics* turned off.
— Pagers, cell phones, and so on are turned off during team meetings.

❑ Decisions are reached by consensus.
— For mission-critical or high buy-in type decisions, pros and cons of alternative approaches will be thoroughly discussed and evaluated until all members come to agreement that they can all support the decision.

❑ Decisions and action items are recorded.
— Decisions and agreed-to action items will be recorded by a volunteer or assigned team member, and distributed to other members prior to the next meeting.

— Action items will include action to be taken, the name of the person assigned responsibility, and the planned completion date.

❑ Previously absent or new members are updated.

— Before team meetings, the team updates a team member who was absent or is new.

## Meeting Effectiveness Check

In the early stages, teams are learning how to be aware of and attend to many things, including:

❑ Team member participation
❑ Team member dominance
❑ Conflict
❑ Meeting efficiency
❑ Meeting location issues
❑ Team meeting management.
    — Ground rules
    — Agendas
    — Action items
    — Start/stop on time.

At the end of every team meeting, a team can gain great benefit from assessing how well the meeting went. About two or three minutes are needed, and the project leader or facilitator should ask two questions:

❑ "What helped this meeting be effective?"
❑ "What hindered the meeting's effectiveness?"

Write down the team members' responses (preferably on a flipchart under headings of "Helped" and "Hindered").

The team should discuss and agree on ways to eliminate or reduce things that hindered the meeting and to reinforce what helped.

At the next meeting, the previous meeting effectiveness check should be reviewed to ensure that *past sins* are not repeated.

## Surfacing Issues Technique

When a project team becomes *bogged down* or *stuck* in a meeting, the following technique can be used by a facilitator or a project leader to surface unstated or undiscussed concerns that are affecting the team's performance:

❑ Ask team members to write on blank three-by-five cards what they think is blocking the team members from working well together, or what has been going on in the team that has not been discussed.

❑ Collect the cards (then have the team take a five-minute break).

❑ Post the items (anonymously) on a flipchart.

❑ Have the team vote or rate each item's impact on the team's success (high, medium, or low).

❑ Have the team discuss the high-impact items openly and come to closure on what the team or specific team members will do to eliminate or reduce the *blockers*.

## Consensus

Teams vote on things to identify priorities or shorten lists of items to discuss.

Teams should *not* vote to make decisions on approaches or recommendations that are critical to successfully achieving the team's mission.

Instead, the team should evaluate the pros and cons of each approach/recommendation, and make sure that everyone's view is heard and that no one is being *sold* or *ramrodded* on a particular view.

Given a thorough discussion, the team then comes to an agreement on which approach/recommendation each member on the team can support or *live with* (probably not each person's first choice, but one that will work given the group's discussion).

It is important to check for consensus by asking any quiet team members if they can support the approach/recommendation on which the team seems to be converging. By carefully ensuring that consensus is reached, the approach/recommendation will be endorsed and supported by every team member during presentations to management and while implementing the approach/recommendation.

# Upgrade Your Project Management Knowledge with First-Class Publications from PMI

## DON'T PARK YOUR BRAIN OUTSIDE
### A PRACTICAL GUIDE TO IMPROVING SHAREHOLDER VALUE WITH SMART MANAGEMENT

*Don't Park Your Brain Outside* is the thinking person's guide to extraordinary project performance. Francis Hartman has assembled a cohesive and balanced approach to highly effective project management. It is deceptively simple. Called SMART, this new approach is Strategically Managed, Aligned, Regenerative, and Transitional. It is based on research and best practices, tempered by hard-won experience. SMART has saved significant time and money on the hundreds of large and small, simple and complex projects on which it has been tested. Are your projects SMART? Find out by reading this people-oriented project management book with an attitude!

ISBN: 1-880410-48-6 (paperback)

## THE ENTERPRIZE ORGANIZATION
### ORGANIZING SOFTWARE PROJECTS FOR ACCOUNTABILITY AND SUCCESS

Every day project leaders are approached with haunting questions like: *What is the primary reason why projects fail? How technical should managers be? What are the duties of a project management office?* These haunting questions, along with many more, are just a few of the question and answers Whitten discusses in his latest book, *The EnterPrize Organization*. This book is for seasoned employees, as well as for those just entering the workforce. From beginning to end,

you will recognize familiar ways to define the key project roles and responsibilities, and discover some new ideas in organizing a software project.

ISBN: 1-880410-79-6 (paperback)

## A FRAMEWORK FOR PROJECT MANAGEMENT

This complete project management seminar course provides experienced project managers with an easy-to-use set of educational tools to help them deliver a seminar on basic project management concepts, tools, and techniques. *A Framework for Project Management* was developed and designed for seminar leaders by a team of experts within the PMI® membership, and reviewed extensively during its development and piloting stage by a team of PMPs.

ISBN: 1-880410-82-6 (Facilitator's Manual Set)
ISBN: 1-880410-80-X (Participant's Manual Set)

## THE PMI PROJECT MANAGEMENT FACT BOOK

A comprehensive resource of information about PMI® and the profession it serves. Professionals working in project management require information and resources to function in today's global business environment. Knowledge along with data collection and interpretation are often key to determining success in the marketplace. The Project Management Institute (PMI®) anticipates the needs of the profession with *The PMI Project Management Fact Book*.

ISBN: 1-880410-62-1 (paperback)

## Project Management Software Survey

The PMI® *Project Management Software Survey* offers an efficient way to compare and contrast the capabilities of a wide variety of project management tools. More than two hundred software tools are listed with comprehensive information on systems features; how they perform time analysis, resource analysis, cost analysis, performance analysis, and cost reporting; and how they handle multiple projects, project tracking, charting, and much more. The survey is a valuable tool to help narrow the field when selecting the best project management tools.
ISBN: 1-880410-52-4 (paperback)
ISBN: 1-880410-59-1 (CD-ROM)

## The Juggler's Guide to Managing Multiple Projects

This comprehensive book introduces and explains task-oriented, independent, and interdependent levels of project portfolios. It says that you must first have a strong foundation in time management and priority setting, then introduces the concept of Portfolio Management to timeline multiple projects, determine their resource requirements, and handle emergencies, putting you in charge for possibly the first time in your life!
ISBN: 1-880410-65-6 (paperback)

## Recipes for Project Success

This book is destined to become "the" reference book for beginning project managers, particularly those who like to cook! Practical, logically developed project management concepts are offered in easily understood terms in a lighthearted manner. They are applied to the everyday task of cooking—from simple, single dishes, such as homemade tomato sauce for pasta, made from the bottom up, to increasingly complex dishes or meals for groups that in turn require an understanding of more complex project management terms and techniques. The transition between cooking and project management discussions is smooth, and tidbits of information provided with the recipes are interesting and humorous.
ISBN: 1-880410-58-3 (paperback)

## Tools and Tips for Today's Project Manager

This guidebook is valuable for understanding project management and performing to quality standards. Includes project management concepts and terms—old and new—that are not only defined but also are explained in much greater detail than you would find in a typical glossary. Also included are tips on handling such seemingly simple everyday tasks as how to say "No" and how to avoid telephone tag. It's a reference you'll want to keep close at hand.
ISBN: 1-880410-61-3 (paperback)

## The Future of Project Management

The project management profession is going through tremendous change—both evolutionary and revolutionary. Some of these changes are internally driven, while many are externally driven. Here, for the first time, is a composite view of some major trends occurring throughout the world and the implication of them on the profession of project management and on the Project Management Institute. Read the views of the 1998 PMI Research Program Team, a well-respected futurist firm, and other authors. This book represents the beginning of a journey and, through inputs from readers and others, it will continue as a work in progress.
ISBN: 1-880410-71-0 (paperback)

## New Resources for PMP Candidates

The following publications are resources that certification candidates can use to gain information on project management theory, principles, techniques, and procedures.

## PMP Resource Package

*Earned Value Project Management*
by Quentin W. Fleming and Joel M. Koppelman

*Effective Project Management: How to Plan, Manage, and Deliver Projects on Time and Within Budget*
by Robert K. Wysocki, et al.

*A Guide to the Project Management
Body of Knowledge (PMBOK® Guide)*
by the PMI Standards Committee

*Human Resource Skills for the Project Manager*
by Vijay K. Verma

*The New Project Management*
by J. Davidson Frame

*Organizing Projects for Success*
by Vijay K. Verma

*Principles of Project Management*
by John Adams, et al.

*Project & Program Risk Management*
by R. Max Wideman, Editor

*Project Management Casebook*
edited by David I. Cleland, et al.

*Project Management: A Managerial Approach,
Fourth Edition*
by Jack R. Meredith and Samuel J. Mantel Jr.

*Project Management: A Systems Approach to
Planning, Scheduling, and Controlling,
Sixth Edition*
by Harold Kerzner

## A GUIDE TO THE PROJECT MANAGEMENT BODY OF KNOWLEDGE (PMBOK® GUIDE)

The basic management reference for everyone
who works on projects. Serves as a tool for
learning about the generally accepted knowledge
and practices of the profession. As "management
by projects" becomes more and more a recom-
mended business practice worldwide, the
*PMBOK® Guide* becomes an essential source of
information that should be on every manager's
bookshelf. Available in hardcover or paperback,
the *PMBOK® Guide* is an official standards document of the Project Management Institute.
ISBN: 1-880410-12-5 (paperback), ISBN: 1-
880410-13-3 (hardcover)

## INTERACTIVE PMBOK® GUIDE

This CD-ROM makes it easy for you to access the
valuable information in PMI's *PMBOK® Guide*.
Features hypertext links for easy reference—
simply click on underlined words in the text, and
the software will take you to that particular
section in the *PMBOK® Guide*. Minimum system
requirements: 486 PC; 8MB RAM; 10MB free disk
space; CD-ROM drive, mouse, or other pointing
device; and Windows 3.1 or greater.

## MANAGING PROJECTS STEP-BY-STEP™

Follow the steps, standards, and procedures used
and proven by thousands of professional project
managers and leading corporations. This interactive multimedia CD-ROM, based on PMI's
*PMBOK® Guide*, will enable you to customize,
standardize, and distribute your project plan standards, procedures, and methodology across your
entire organization. Multimedia illustrations using
3-D animations and audio make this perfect for
both self-paced training or for use by a facilitator.

## PMBOK® Q&A

Use this handy pocket-sized question-and-answer
study guide to learn more about the key themes
and concepts presented in PMI's international
standard, *PMBOK® Guide*. More than 160
multiple-choice questions with answers (refer-
enced to the *PMBOK® Guide*) help you with the
breadth of knowledge needed to understand key
project management concepts.
ISBN: 1-880410-21-4 (paperback)

## PMI PROCEEDINGS LIBRARY CD-ROM

This interactive guide to PMI's annual Seminars &
Symposium proceedings offers a powerful new
option to the traditional methods of document
storage and retrieval, research, training, and technical writing. Contains complete paper presentations from PMI '92–PMI '97 with full-text search
capability, convenient onscreen readability, and
PC/Mac compatibility.

## PMI PUBLICATIONS LIBRARY CD-ROM

Using state-of-the-art technology, PMI offers complete articles and information from its major publications on one CD-ROM, including *PM Network* (1990–97), *Project Management Journal* (1990–97), and *A Guide to the Project Management Body of Knowledge*. Offers full-text search capability and indexing by *PMBOK® Guide* knowledge areas. Electronic indexing schemes and sophisticated search engines help to quickly find and retrieve articles that are relevant to your topic or research area.

## *ALSO AVAILABLE FROM PMI*

**Project Management for Managers**
Mihály Görög, Nigel J. Smith
ISBN: 1-880410-54-0 (paperback)

**Project Leadership: From Theory to Practice**
Jeffery K. Pinto, Peg Thoms, Jeffrey Trailer, Todd Palmer, Michele Govekar
ISBN: 1-880410-10-9 (paperback)

**Annotated Bibliography of Project and Team Management**
David I. Cleland, Gary Rafe, Jeffrey Mosher
ISBN: 1-880410-47-8 (paperback)
ISBN: 1-880410-57-5 (CD-ROM)

**How to Turn Computer Problems into Competitive Advantage**
Tom Ingram
ISBN: 1-880410-08-7 (paperback)

**Achieving the Promise of Information Technology**
Ralph B. Sackman
ISBN: 1-880410-03-6 (paperback)

**Leadership Skills for Project Managers**
Editors' Choice Series
Edited by Jeffrey K. Pinto, Jeffrey W. Trailer
ISBN: 1-880410-49-4 (paperback)

**The Virtual Edge**
Margery Mayer
ISBN: 1-880410-16-8 (paperback)

**The ABCs of DPC**
Edited by PMI's Design-Procurement-Construction Specific Interest Group
ISBN: 1-880410-07-9 (paperback)

**Project Management Casebook**
Edited by David I. Cleland, Karen M. Bursic, Richard Puerzer, A. Yaroslav Vlasak
ISBN: 1-880410-45-1 (paperback)

**Project Management Casebook Instructor's Manual**
Edited by David I. Cleland, Karen M. Bursic, Richard Puerzer, A. Yaroslav Vlasak
ISBN: 1-880410-18-4 (paperback)

**The PMI Book of Project Management Forms**
ISBN: 1-880410-31-1 (paperback)
ISBN: 1-880410-50-8 (diskette version)

**Principles of Project Management**
John Adams et al.
ISBN: 1-880410-30-3 (paperback)

**Organizing Projects for Success**
Human Aspects of Project Management Series, Volume 1
Vijay K. Verma
ISBN: 1-880410-40-0 (paperback)

**Human Resource Skills for the Project Manager**
Human Aspects of Project Management Series, Volume 2
Vijay K. Verma
ISBN: 1-880410-41-9 (paperback)

**Managing the Project Team**
Human Aspects of Project Management Series, Volume 3
Vijay K. Verma
ISBN: 1-880410-42-7 (paperback)

**Earned Value Project Management**
Quentin W. Fleming, Joel M. Koppelman
ISBN: 1-880410-38-9 (paperback)

**Value Management Practice**
Michel Thiry
ISBN: 1-880410-14-1 (paperback)

**Decision Analysis in Projects**
John R. Schuyler
ISBN: 1-880410-39-7 (paperback)

# Order online at
# www.pmibookstore.org

## Book Ordering Information

Phone: 412.741.6206
Fax: 412.741.0609
Email: pmiorders@abdintl.com

Mail: PMI Publications Fulfillment Center
     PO Box 1020
     Sewickley, Pennsylvania 15143-1020 USA